T0316470

THE
TIME PIECE

CAMBRIDGE
UNIVERSITY PRESS

University Printing House, Cambridge CB2 8BS, United Kingdom

Cambridge University Press is part of the University of Cambridge.

It furthers the University's mission by disseminating knowledge in the pursuit of education, learning and research at the highest international levels of excellence.

www.cambridge.org
Information on this title: www.cambridge.org/9781107586123

First published 1945
First paperback edition 2015

A catalogue record for this publication is available from the British Library

ISBN 978-1-107-58612-3 Paperback

The

TIME PIECE

A Poem

BY

FRANK KENDON

" How great is that darkness"

CAMBRIDGE

At the University Press

1945

To

GERALD
BULLETT

The
TIME PIECE

[I]

Past midnight, but the night as dark as night;
The said twelvemonth accepting ritual death
While night looks on, and expectation sinks
To ash again. We need not mend this fire.

Past zero of the year. Among his stars
The dark hand wanders. No committal bell
Declares midwinter with a deep and dying stroke;
The brother of space has silence for a bell.

Past midnight, with the night starry and black
And constant in its journey, in its sleep.
No Eye to notice, while we mount to rest,
Hurtled through shadow on successive stairs,
Or in still dream, or bedded with mock thought,
Moving vastly away through virgin space.

The clockmaker commends another year.
Begins no year, none ends, but our rehearsal,
As we wait eagerly on the wide river
Where brings time's true and everlasting tide

New disposition for our plaything senses.
Spent is the past. A bell can nowise age us.
Set down the glasses on their rings again.
To bed, this year. We are halfway, are moving.
A frozen night; no moon.

[II]

Sometimes even
Cold for no symbol can be perfect when,
    Aloft in noble trees,
Silence is frozen white among the branches there,
Before the astonisht sun—a speechless witness,
Such that he who can believe the rime he sees
    Can believe anything.

[III]

Does not my diagram show that spinning earth
Makes day and night; that, rolling in her girth
Along an orbit pivoted upon
The unconsuming and inflaming sun,
She stems a fraction of his radial heat,
And with each circuit scores a year complete?
Show should it also how, by curious chance—
An axis tilted—this unending dance

Gathers variety not at all implied
In star-born symmetry. (And this divide
The good to seasons, on a calendar,
And teach the surge and subsidence of a year.)
Diagram shows no goodman; earth, asleep,
Knows nothing of the fourfold plan we keep;
Of frost, of sap, of swath, of fruit, she hears
Nothing as down her destind track she veers.
Nor does the sun, this ball which hovers, burning,
As if to watch earth's wheel of nothing turning,
Pouring a wasteful flood through wantless space,
One ray of which finds hindrance at her face.
Sun loves not earth; earth feels not us, her creatures;
Ants and stars have their proportiond natures:
Stars and suns, it seems, forever to shine and move,
And Lives, not shining, living by hate and love.
O then, Philosopher, boast not gift unfairly:
In midst of trees, valleys, and waters born,
To these must life begin outpouring early;
It is not science sanctifies each morning,
But that within, which hails the sun an angel;
No diagram, no proof—a wild evangel,
Whose needy believers, cheerd by a glance of light,
Make spring of winter gaily, morning of night.

[IV]

Here winter aconites among wet beech leaves
Pois'd to gaze between iron bars to the sky...

Who told them Time's as yet unpublisht legend?
Oh, how far down do tender fibres extend
Unto what stronghold in what merciful dark
That flowers outface unalterable No?

Suppose they are sure by patience of their nature,
Took dying easily, mourn'd not to forget,
Seek not now in vain to surpass themselves—

[V]

Come, daybreak hope, to passive cold despair,
Finger the curtain with life-giving air.
Over wide lands from lethargy now lift us,
Lean survivors all of winter's thrift.
We part the folds; we would, through mortal frost,
See that begin which has of late almost
Died from these dreamless ways. They shall behold
Our tiles and tree-top edges afloat with gold.
O let it be bright, and bring—and melt thereby—
Tears that are not tears to our wakening eyes.

8

A thrush sings nearer now. His beacon calls,
Sweeping stale night away, shall break the walls,
Wrench off the bolts of darkness, and, for a new creation,
Unbind our bodies and mend our meditation...
Come, daybreak, daybreak to passive cold despair,
Finger the curtain with life-giving air.

[VI]

Needy we are, but not unfortunate;
For this remote king of heaven whom we await
(A clot of fire, incapable of folly)
Both winter melts and our long melancholy.

    Seeds first and spores catch life at his sphere's fire;
Birds by his beams are voiced with their desire;
Buds their vanes spread at touches of his terror;
Meek mind itself warms passion at his mirror;
For him butterflies creep from a dusty hiding;
Rooks here this first wet vernal gale outriding
Charge down his streaming sunbeams over the fallows;
And starveling age bends onward, talking of swallows.

9

These kin as a god the furious Sunstar wakens.
He pours himself down. What's to him who takes
His light for virtue, his expense as gift?
Earth knows not, even, in her headlong drift,
How spring begins in wight and weed and beast—
Why dawn gets earlier welcome in the east.

[VII]

Hold out your palms to the rains that fall, in March
When the daffodils bluster here and there under trees;
We are waiting our cue from these impatient ones.

The clouds drive over, fringed with welcome water;
We can leave the fire; we are proof against the cold,
Cloakt with our mounting expectancy, while still
The mercury stands at winter, and a thread
Scarcely shows in the soil that was winter mud.

And, by their songs, the birds themselves are like us,
Glad to survive and eager to be alive,
Powerful death-forgetters; channels as we
Of the jet of spirit that flouts mortality...

The wheat thrusts gaily up through the crumbled furrow,
And the rain that darkens the furrow
Washes its blades to their right and sturdy green,
Kind to a farmer's eyes. A shepherd stoops
To the ewe with her lamb in the sheltering hurdle of straw;
The level wind tosses the grainless ears;
The dog stands, dreaming to north, bearing the gale.

[VIII]

Stillness is not silence; there is more
Than silence working. Over the far fields,
Tidy table-lands furrowd in corduroy,
One degree, one kindly degree more warm,
And a knowledge that brings keen vision (perhaps a folly
For candlelight eyes) in prophecy wanders afield,
Disturbing the flocks of plover, which seek to settle,
But ever fly keening, wheeling, turning, mounting,
Peopling the air with wanton and delay...
What is it we search for, with bewilderd need,
In silver-white of sky, and brown of the fields?
One somewhere seen among the willows in mist,
Who does not know she is mistress of so many.

By the little streams we went, my daughter and I,
One polish'd easter day, when wide and high
Was the dome, and deep the blue, of the cloudless ceiling.
Piercing clear, clean and keen was the light
Entring the wavy glass of the softly-stealing—
A day of blue and gold, of each so bright
That our eyes wrinkld against the blade of the light,
Marking with pleasure how the shadows curvd
Across the brass-bound osier boughs and branches.
And I, I recall, had happen'd to look at the sun
At the selfsame time when she set eyes upon
The first marsh marigold budding against the bridge.
She shouted it out to me; but I was hinder'd—
Blind with unbidden suns of blue and crimson,
Which mockt my vision, and dazzled quite from my sight
Her strong green witness of a good beginning.
Soon, however, my secret astronomy falter'd;
The purple suns floated down the stream;
And I saw the spring before me as she had seen it.
We did not gather the bud (so to destroy it)
But left it, leaning both in sole possession
Over the solid rail of our brief bridge.

If bidden, oh then before the beginning of Time
Bidden to waste, in a frenzy of incandescence,
The obedient Sun wakens this twig of lime....
Earth, who darkly hovers about his presence,
Now at this point in heaven intercepteth
At a warm slant once more his outward fever—
Whereat beast, man, and tree, her life-adepts,
By those waves kisst, takes each a step that never
Never to the end of Time will be retraced.
Now new buds fatten, now the dumb hope cries
Leaves, wings, to quicken this lost paradise—
On earth which wanders—while sun flames to waste.

   O Unheard, Unhearing! Given this gold
Our griefs disrobe to life, our chrysalids unfold.

[XI]

By blackbirds' bowings to brown mistresses
I rede there will be nests along these hedges.
We shall go out, one shouting winter day
(The ship clouds sailing steadily all one way,
Wheeling the spokes of sunbeams swift and wide
Over the land set free)

And by the layerd edge of this woodside
We'll suddenly stop near by; stand, stooping over
To see the dark throat pulsing, the still eye
Fixt fast in fearful courage; hear the cry
As terror gets the mastery, and she threads
Down through the thorns away.
Then shall we stoop our heads
Above the tangle—there in the warm cup
Find four or five bright eggs—and go our ways
Foolishly lifted up as if by hope.
While she, when we be safely out of range,
Will creep beneath the thorns in passionate doubt,
Find the eggs safe, and nestle them like pain
To the warm comfort of her body pressd,
Drawing the ache of motherhood back again.

[XII]

Young William's out by wood side, watchful and shy,
Avoiding humans, not quite willing why,
But in a sweat of diffidence, to cover,
This phantasy of himself as Emily's lover.

She may be about; yet either he'd be dumb,
Or talk foolish, should she happen to come.
Or if tonight she come not, then he'll be
Madly humble for hoping as high as she.

What chant is this? What magnet in whose field
We tremble and struggle and resent, and yield?
What's *like*, to make a fool of manly reason?
Why does strong mind surrender to such treason?
What bides, if will itself can be thus swayd
By the mere namesake of a milky maid?

Stand still, young culprit: half a universe
Puts you about, to cross your path with hers.

[XIII]

I saw them, single proud and defiant,
On watch as if for an ambusht enemy,
Reard above their clustering shields
In fixt and fearless mien;
Yet of innocent influence,
Swaying softly against the incessant
Youthful air, which rustles the rattling drift
Forgotten since autumn's fall.

15

Or now, at point and ecstasy of their pleasure,
Asking and offering serious delight;
Darkly for dealer bees alert,
And cheapening, by anguisht simplicity,
Honey, for offspring.

By a strange unlikeness,
Before their sculptur'd passion
We know our livelong neighbour-hood:
That tender sorry joy, divided delicately,
Of holy fragrance and defiant lightness;

How, madly demanding comely continuance,
Above all other earthly benefit
Kind values its own;
In some to petal flowers climbing,
In some to a lover's lover's bow'd solicitude,
In some to a silver laughter in the shadow;
Liking, or flower, or curve of life's access
More than the need, unnecessarily lovely,
A bye-worship, promise delaying fulfilment—
Desire, the care-taker with angel countenance,
Or fierce violet informd and fashiond with patience
And a custom of holy breath.

[XIV]

The rain's done, the sky clear, the wind abroad;
The stream's full, the verge gold, the acre ploughed;
The day's new, the air fresh, the heart high—
Proves nothing. Wager nothing. Ask not. Stand by.
So do such waifs as primroses; yet every year
Brings banks of light to doorsteps of despair.

[XV]

The blossom tassell'd on its thousand trees;
The orchard, roof'd with cloud, tufted with these
Five-petall'd purities the cherry-flowers;
The sculptur'd boughs, the crystal hours, Recall;
Th' intense dark vault, the holy scent, the sun,
The dazzl'd dusty lanes that twist and run
By banks ahead, and creep and crisp and rise
Full of hot silence under easter skies.

Behind the pleated leaves of hazel rods,
Near to the one dog-violet where it nods
At root of silver ladysmocks upstanding
Amid the rusted leaves of lost last year,

17

Find the first wren's nest, built of leaves and moss,
By excess of fire, and now a prodigal loss,
His first unfinisht place, his practice home,
A fallen cherry-flower upon its dome....

One day each spring, a precipice of Time,
Crowds thus this tale and tells it at a breath;
One hour, when sense and spirit, met to bless
The mortal mouth, undo the kiss of death.
We'll get no wiser with our sceptic care:
God's life, man's would-be-good, the Spring, is here;
And now we kneel, for no unheeding sun
Burns in his void, a told phenomenon.

[XVI]

'The trees resolving first to bud and be,
The bank's despair transform'd itself to fronds.
Now that the thorn, now that the apple tree
Shake down their light and loosen their soft sounds,
Now that the lock'd-in watersprings unlink
And laugh and hurry along, and leap and sparkle,

And noiseless rere-mice stammer across the dark
Of moonlit leas with moonlit buttercups sprinkl'd,
I call on you, five mortal wits, to make
A madrigal together, *One Day's Ending*:—
Thorn-blossom twilight—coolness on your cheek—
A scent, though sweet, that has a meaning in it—
The taste of prophecy in rain dew-risen.
Now, in this thick shade, one yielded minute,
See touch taste smell the nearness of the season,
Then hear my cry, a line across the silence,
Giving the wildness of the wood its right,
Piercing the fog of beauty clear with reason...'

This, from a nightingale alone last night,
(It is a summer theme)
Which by zeal of passion and by skill of quiet
And by folded wings
Breeds the resolve it brings.

Courtship with spring is over; summer, mated,
Stands serious-eyed upon her threshold—yours.
Make of this world from now what must be made—
Good use by wedlock, while the gracious hours
Of daylight lengthen, that your destin'd tasks
May be continued and brought on to fruit.
Outlive the ironies of dazzl'd blindness;
Here's rays to use, here's purpose to take root.
Swink in the total sunshine, stoop to spade,
Stoop to make fat the soil, to sow, to choose,
To fence the weeds outside, to pour the water;
Keep favourites ruthlessly; put love to use.
Prodigal life will fast outrun your hand.
Good husbands must be firm, when wives command.

She stands thigh-deep in foam of flowery kex,
Her skirts yet girt for the work her strength has finisht,
Summer, with hand at eyebrows looking far
Across her southern farm.

So stood she as I pass'd; but me she saw not;
As I lookt back she stood so, living onward,
Watching far off where by a woodland gap
Her leisurely cattle, chanted to stall and stool,
Stroll'd through the haze and stept into sombre barns
Standing asleep in the kingdom of afternoon.

[XIX]

My neighbour bets and drinks, but I do neither;
Yet when, after a long spell of dry weather,
The rain soaks down and lays the drifted dust,
It shows no favour to unjust or just.

How complicated, but for this, would be
The elements of meteorology;
And but for this, how straight and simple would
Our judgment be of who is bad, or good.

Summer, like thought, goes quiet about her work.
The ten continuing strokes from the sunlit belfry
Run tingling through the street from end to end,
And like as not meet nobody coming or going;
For the men are far afield, and the wives indoors.

Now silenced children, usher'd and demure,
Rang'd in a diaper-pattern of solitude
(Lonely in company, pensive or submissive),
Hear Ten come laggards down, and learn how slowly
The ancient years of Bible history change.
The window-panes of school, the teaching echoes,
The iron taste of ink, the sombre sameness,
These are their victuals, have been so, they think,
Since Solomon's day. They scarcely hope as yet
An end to this long morning; do not know
That on the floor the south-east sunsquares creep
From spot to stain, through spelling, writing, sums.
But creaking Time, steept in his belfry tower,
Watchful, constant, uneager, docks their durance.
Eleven opens and dies; the hour goes under;
And next, of a sudden, with lawless quarters jangling,
Down come the golden Dozen. Lessons end.

Now doors swing out to white reality—
The dazzling street, the basking shopkeepers,
The sweating smith, the geese beyond the church,
The fifty paths for home. . . . They scatter wide
Carrying their treble voices here and far
By bridleways and stiles and past the shade
Of apple trees to many gates, until
The dreamer last gets home, expected so . . .

And a waggoner—the cue that quiet waited—
Turns his ribbon'd team towards the shade,
Himself goes thirsty in . . . But all that hour,
About the hush of dinner-time, in secret,
The subtle tedium of Time is turning;
And when four-quarters sounds again—and soon—
Snail-pace light, and a close but different air,
Will bring, as Afternoon, a lazier gloom.

So still in the garden the tulips
Are standing. Not a breath shakes
The butterfly leaves of the pear-tree,
Or loosens the flakes
Of the cherry, or bends the tops
Of grass in the gilded meadow,
Where rises and drops
A milkwhite butterfly
Under a cloudless sky.

Aimless, this endless morning,
The dew cold to my wrist,
I have lain in the shadow, watching,
And still the mist
Of daybreak veils the gray hills,
And above the motionless meadow
Warmth distils.
Earth, are you real? Am I?
In whose dream do we exist?
What means this passionless sky?

[XXII]

Close your wrinkl'd eyes....
Listen....In this tale
Leaves mesh and maze
Mile beyond mile;
Under sultry noon
Larks rise and roam,
From whom ring and sprinkle
Clear cones of song.

In the sacred woods,
In the breathless heat,
Each sound recedes,
Faints and falls mute;
And ever wakes other where
Haze-haunted echo,
Headlong, deep and pure,
The placeless cuckoo.

Idly may the blind
Touch perpetual Now;
Time becomes a sound—
Far-off and nigh—
Arch'd on these meads,

Noon's oxeye acres
Hush'd under drowsy trades
Of Noon's honey-seekers,

Less than a sigh from the leaves to hear,
Or of roseleaves falling behind us;
Slowly has shade that screen'd us, shifting,
Stol'n to the sunburn'd hives.
What would avail my gaze, your labour?
In time summer overwhelms all kind;
Underneath hush, each root, each fibre,
Is harvest—its last least berry—plann'd.

[XXIII]

This child is the lovely child
Of the fang'd wild rose—
His fairest heiress—
Summer's true newcomer,
Which suddenly o'erblows
Our June hedgerows.

So fiercely father'd
She will never be gather'd—
Even at gentlest touch
May seldom be taken
No petal downshaken.

Much, then, not to clutch
For a pleasure such treasure—
Nor trespass to possess
Such delicateness.

Who may scorn thorns
Her fragility mourns:
More so than fresh wounds
In hurt, hasty hands.

Pray, wayfarer, spare her,
Look lowly upon her;
Incense not her innocence,
Best self-possess'd;
Hush breath on her honour.

Thus alone is preserv'd
Her tense, curv'd quiet,
In gentle memory lapt,
Kind in the mind.

Moreover, to leave her so,
Though for another lover,
Has one heart assur'd
Forever full reward.

Today she stays awhile—
Tomorrow she goes—
This child, this the lovely child
Of the fang'd wild rose.

[XXIV]

The brazen midweek days are plied with work.
The mornings are too short to be rememberd
When the straight burning fingers of the sun
Already high on his way, by curtain cheating,
Search for reluctant lashes, to steal under.
On attic walls the throbbing bricks drink deep
Of early light and warmth; at the back door
All that is left of dayspring's coolness shrivels
From a fierce taskmaster's eye among the leaves.
Dawn was a brief legend. This is noon of the year.

The mountain-slope of every crumb of soil
Is bright and chalky; ants have walking shadows;
Dust smokes at every strike of the hoe.

   There can be no escape from this fierce pressure;
Neither may eyes be raised, nor sweat allayd,
Nor refuge found from surly heat, in barn,
Or under trees, or by the diminishing pond,
Or even indoors. The rays pour straitly down
Upon our one enormous disk of land,
The sunflower kingdom. Far across the brook
Field beyond field beyond field of standing crops,
With flicker of heat and flicker of butterfly wing,
Stretches away to woods which, smalld to scrub,
Falter and move and melt upon horizons.
Nothing but fact by fact is true, in this black light:
Day going on as day, as day declining;
And Summer herself, bent home to a daylit pallet,
Dust-clad, dog-tired, dreamless beneath the elms....

   Ah, but tonight the omen leaves hang still;
The rooks come raggedly home;
For the first of forgotten clouds builds up by half-light
Low in the manifold north its thundering dome.

She frown'd at work next day and would not speak;
Small and far afield she stopt her hoe,
Lean'd on it often, looking up, distracted,
To the piling clouds, which blurr'd the edge of light
But drugg'd the whole day with imprisoning heat.
Not a bird was seen or sang; the aspens stopp'd...
But about evening time she laid aside
Her working garments with her working mind
And climb'd, renew'd, the turf-skinn'd tumulus,
Till she trod far above the grave-lined plain.
There, time and space looked youngly back at her;
And Summer nobly stood above all things,
Grave as granite, gentle as love not speaking.

[XXVI]

Some cottage child in a valley must have seen
The pale flash leap behind the clouds, when Summer
Lifting her mind above the imprisoning land
Let fall her hoe and harness. But at first

30

As nightfall darkened, as the city of clouds
Spread from the south, immovably enlarging,
The weather-wisest scarcely yet foresaw
What majesty was threatened. Even stars
Looked undaunted down from eastern heaven;
Only the blue air, still and listening,
An image of cool starlight, but no more,
Could not abate night's close and heavy heat.
The weariest, all, were wakeful—man and bird
And beast were wakeful—while by star and star
The sluggish darkness of great cloud crept higher—
Once a wind spun suddenly, whipped the trees
So that they cried, and in the night it seemed
One saw imploring arms and straining roots—
But failed and died away as suddenly
Thereafter; and, in stranger silence sunken,
The clock below struck off one endless hour.

The day began amiss, a stifling night,
A restless sleep, a dawn without a sun;
Grey meal on hedge, a ceiling at the treetop,
Silence, birdless, waterless, thick and fell.

What day can hold this mood all day unbroken,
But threshing soon his oaken limbs, in wrath
Must rise and mutter of tempest of disquiet,
With floods and fire to purge his fever off?

Run, ants, to save, while yet the gust arises,
Your dry dry-weather toys; Wives, within doors,
Upstairs and roundabout, make fast your windows,
Cover the knives and mirrors... That's the first
Far-away grumble in the southern lands;
Shudder of yielding with that groan gave warning,
Whereat the quick gleam above languisht away.

Dun smoke, dark boiling dross, roofs-in the ruin;
Our pitiful land is at disaster; a Thing,
A Being with sinews of striving air, seizes,
Takes in his arms, our venerable trees;
Their leaves he tears by twigs wildly away;
They run with whirlwinds into the corner's dust.

Each elm-tree grimly holds his cap on his head,
Struggles to wrap his whistling garments closer
About his stubborn trunk. Dumb in the din
A vagabond, halfway between nights' dosses,
Clutching his rags, looks quickly round, but dares
No shelter take; the long wind drives him on.
A door slams. Echoes empty the house...

This, three of us upon the threshold hearing—
Three selves transfigured (though we knew it not)
Came forth to watch. But each had part in that
Whose reckless life was readable in ours—
In dark strength, and in tumult of passions,
The soul of Nature knew, and we in her,
Like exaltation from an unknown source...

Rain cannot fall for tempesting. Those gnarld
And obstinate old thorn trees well may cry—
May bow, may twist, and chafe their knotted hands—
Crash! She gets nearer! Westward the last slot
Of the last gleam of daylight closes down;
Gloom in a gradual instant darkens afield.
Oh, run in! Take any sort of door
Run—*Crash!*—Oh, noble noble!

Even the roses have forced their heads away;
Leaves of the ivy lift their thousand hands
And make a shivering rush of supplication.
Now all noise dies; now into widening silence
The climax hesitates, the boughs withdrawing.

We question each, with sidelong upward look,
Whether the stroke returns, or we be cheated;
And a shower comes running hither across the road.
Then with a stealthy hiss, a mounting roar,
The downfall tells the tonnage of the rain.
Instantly a water-scented coolness
Washes in. We drink, with nostrils wide;
The gullies flood, the little gravel leaps,
The borders darken. Underneath the throb
A disappointed sullen thunder drums,
And faltering moves afar. Such weight of rain,
We know, and wager, cannot continue long—
It beats a mist of spray above the ground,
Is never constant, but now batters down
Fiercely, and now from roar to whip deceases;
Till we, being spellbound by its force, draw in
A hiss of sudden horror, for a sere
Blackening brilliance rips the welkin across,

Quivering stands in every arrested rod
And separate bead of solid rain...at which
Spirits lie empty, that the brittle crack
And dark downfall of thunderclap on heels
Of light may render conscious life again.
Here, still alive, though out of reach of speech,
Annihilated, yet found swiftly anew,
We know what worship is; the weakest wits
Are teachable; and awe can hallow fear.

The rain is relenting. Passion and weight of the fall
Quickly expended, now to soft shower changing,
Scatters a dust of water into the air,
A sweet forgiving sprinkle, venturable.
The coolness, too, as of our clothes translating,
Is live and fair, and stands at open window
And door beckoning us. If rooms are stale,
The more our range is lightning, lightness, richness,
Freedom, certainty; and with one accord
We watchers set our foot and courage forth
And take possession, boldly entering earth.

Now, indeed, after tumult, the bowers
Of leaves hang quiet, heavy and full fed;

The grass can drink no moisture more; and purer
Than maiden spring the summer's flowers, new dy'd
By the hard rain, and with their veins re-charg'd,
In cooler vigour by submission slumber—
So do upfolded daisies where they lie
In clasp of grass whose greenness bears no likeness.

  New-made, we also wander seeking, finding,
Strange floods, the fresh cut valleys in each dyke,
The doubled herbage. When, with gentle lift
Of troubled clouds, from cleavage in the west
Eve's level light steals out to housetop height,
Repainting with extravagance our fresh
Sight of the good estate of which unwarnd
We are inheritors, new come to our own.

Doubtless we may (with cause) despair, go blind,
Sorrow this world again, make blank with tears
The forthright bold irrelevance of nature;
But, for one witness (and, I think, for three)
Because of this new creature, this high outrage,
This manifest and indiscriminate majesty—
Because of earth's renewed virginity
Whose health and hue and virtue sprang from passion,
Ever is praise in storms, mirth, bravery, frenzy,

Freedom, music, and mastery of love.
Love with his lightning gains on deity.
Mortal little we matter, men, yet strangely
Will storm across our dream a guess of greatness.

[XXVIII]

The hilly counties, with their streams and orchards,
And secret ponds and lanes and scatterd woods,
Are sun-and-shadow-arbours, by the cuckoo
Morning-haunted, when from oak to oak in sojourn,
He passes time above the featherd grasses,
Still only a voice to schoolboys, still in June unknown.

The level counties, with their long perspectives,
Vast skies, breathless acres, lie abroad
Under another and more lordly master
For whom summer is vaulted, hard and clear
From east to west, lacking the fret of trees.

The arbours stir with sheep; or cattle dream
Beside their shade-hung pools; and streams can sing
Even in drought in their dense twilit channels;

But on the naked plains stands daylight tall and lonely,
And along wafting acres not a creature
Flaws the monotony, corn, corn and sky.

The people of the plains have never seen
Black acorns break the circle of full moon;
The people of the arbours do not know
From how far off the homeless packs of clouds,
That parcel out the sky,
Have travelld in their progress—seldom know
How plainsmen may, by levelling their eyes,
Live into sunset off their strip of soil.

The people of the plains have never heard
The woods make whisper with a million leaves,
When a fair breeze, come wandering from the coast,
Stoops to a noon-held valley, bringing breath
And blessing, and a sound recalling rain—

But where a man is born he plants his heart.

Will summer never bate this on-and-on?—
Time-present fuses into memory,
The immediate moment instantly withdrawn
Fades to remoter, brighter obscurity.
Will summer never end this by-and-by?—
Time's self informs her tree-top hidden dove
Whose smoothly spoken warm monotony,
Unenvious of our sleep, dreams on above.
Will summer never end? Nor clock tell true
The nearing term of all these endless lives,
Nor calendar exact, nor tax fall due?

One dewy daybreak came the rattling knives,
Began to crop in swath on swath the grass,
Sorrel and oxeye, quaking-weed and clover,
While horse and mare went sadly trudging over.
They nod to number-up their steps; they pass
Across the unfastened gateway near the lane,
Edge at the angle, lean upon their strength,
Follow the meadow round by breadth and length,
And from hot distance now approach again.
Thus wall by wall the quivering citadel
Without resistance is encroacht upon—
The kingdom of the butterflies is falling—

Soon earliest windrows wilt beneath the sun
And from their fading breathes a honey'd smell
Loaded with memory, yet beyond recalling—
The kingdom of the butterflies is falling;
The tide is turning; harvest has begun.

[xxx]

With lifted heads, with level backs, tails flying
Three foals in paddock show their grace and breeding,
Their young hooves doggedly thudding the closecropt turf
Hither come thundering, stepping forth from delight,
Over the pond-side knoll, round by the pyramid holly,
Up to the top of the slope, far off, where the fence begins.
There, to a sudden standstill fetch'd, they front the wind,
Wild as the wind and proud in poise by nature,
And whinny above brisk wildernesses of reeds
To the distant hissing hushing and narrow sea.

And the patient mares stand dreaming by the water.
Till one, the dark one—loosening her strong neck,
Drops her skull, lips the faultless mirror,

And draws a steady, cool, sustaining drench;
Thence raising lazily that dripping muzzle again,
Workless and wise, the noble careworn head
Rejoins a doze she scarcely interrupted.

And ringlets on the glassy water widen away from her
Flagging softly among the weeds and diamond dragonflies.

[XXXI]

You should wander once from your snug bed of custom,
Cheat the body of sleep for wherewithal
To estrange yourself. Rise, and clothed in silence,
Turning away from reasonable companion,
Tread the midnight stairway, feel your way
In dark ignorance over familiar boards.
So step from the unsuspected jail, and, loosed from comfort,
Meet the cold wave of manless moonlight alone.

Here is that world we outlawed for our peace,
A thought too mighty, too untimely-minded
For us to bear more glances than we must.
Leave the black trees their gestures, leave the eaves

And shapes of kindness, leave the neighbour road
Whose stony talk is friendship, take the open,
Board the wide secresy; and under night
In strange latitudes stand, the star-pricks wheeling
High above in unfamiliar version,
The Plough at nadir, Cassiopeia slung
Sideways in the sky. Bring nothing there
But all-humiliating emptiness;
For light to read use wonder, hunger, fear.
Then, having bathed, baptised in ignorance,
Having, I say, stood still against the wings
Of heaven and what is meant by hell, let sink
A star into the iris of remembrance,
Touch a leaf in brotherhood, and turn
For home again. But never blab of this;
Say, rather, you went out last night alone—
You could not sleep—you walked across the fields
And back again. Those may know who will.

There comes with August inescapably
Some outward change to match an inward mood:
The summer flowers of their abundance falter;
The meadows, well content to lose by scythe
What must in weeks by death have been invaded,
Now press rich aftermath among the stubble,
Verdure flooding through the clipt, raked parchment,
And yearlings browse there, shaggy, red as blood,
Liking the tender grass's perseverance
And thriving on it hugely.

                                Then arrives
The proof of August, wayside meadowsweet;
With purple loosestrife in the watercourses,
And teazels, ringed by zones of lavender, set
In a green fort of spines, but busily overtrodden
By hasty bees;
And, in the hedges, staggering honeysuckle,
And paper-petalled bramble-flowers recalling
The canker-rose that gave June's character.
Hawkweeds begin now—, dandelions decline—
Blood-budded sinjins' wort with pinprickt leaves,
Coarse hogweed for reminder of cowparsley

(A foaming sea in memory, quickly come and gone)
And tawny alexanders: poppies, also,
Carelessly dressed in crowds, and, thus assertive,
Unsung for slender line and well-hung buds;
Hard-headed knapweeds, every knop a cauldron
Of crimson flames upspringing; agrimony
A silent rocket; 'scarlet' pimpernel,
(A colour that has never found a name)
To which, were we but one foot high, we might
Fetch friends, and share our wonder with them gladly.

Haytime is wholly done; but harvest dallies;
Thereby creeps forth, of Saturdays and Sundays,
The labourer turned angler, calm, undevious,
Who'll stand all day, a derrick for a string,
Watching for tiny silver circles, watching
For riding silver ripples, where his float
Suspends the barb, that bears the worm, that writhes
Before the lazy carp, beneath the lily leaves.

There sits or stands this image of a man.
No one comes or goes.
Or if one should, the angler's dream evades him,
(If dream it be, not some mysterious foretaste

Of everlastingness). For some have passed
These stationary individuals,
Lost in forenoon shadow on the other bank,
And gone twelve hours upon time-doggéd errands
Only to find them there, in gaze and pose,
And dream, perhaps, and age, it seems, unchanged;
And even at dusk reluctant to go home.

Waterlilies regard them with tranquility;
Dragonflies hover and vanish near their floats;
Morning swells out to golden noon about them,
And noon deflates to gentle afternoon;
Still and hot and silent breathes their day,
Sinks rosily to never-ending twilight,
When a great star,
Breaking the shell at last,
Melts on the westward water's doubled sky....
And then, at some such taking, will the angler stir,
His line reeled in, his jointed rod dismembered,
And turn through the undergrowth and hide away
Down crackling paths, and trespass safely home.

There was an angler once, one of these men,
Who had a nightmare;
A waterlily from his window seen—
She was a bud upon the pool of midnight,
Narrow-pointed, ominous with promise,
Of unremitting beauty—which he saw
Begin to unbud before his haunted eyes.
The sepals opened like a crack in the door,
The secret whiteness, pure as light itself,
Shone through the slits, and widened steadfastly,
He could not choose but watch. The beauty grew,
Painfully dazzling to his terrified eyes.
The bud became a chalice, at its rim
A crown of gothic petals burning white
Into the chasm of dark, and still she moved—
Broadened from chalice slowly to a cup,
Increasing as she opened, till he knew
The fatal Absolute could not long delay.
Stricken, he clenched his lids, but by that time
The lily mocked at blindness; emanations
Of her angelic shining pierced his temples;
And his Soul he could not clench. . . .

I know the man: I know his wondering children,
His wise and welcome wife, his happy house.
Among all these he stumbles through his days,
Eats, sleeps, and works, as in a golden dream;
Can see a sunset in an insect's wings, he mutters,
Mirth in marigolds; and, in hardwood trees
(By his behaviour—for he speaks but little)
He worships dryads...No one calls so mild
And peaceable a fellow wild in wits,
And only he himself knows that he's mad.

[XXXIV]

Sweep, sweep, sweep away
The dally long of Summer's Day;
Stone on steel, steel on stone,
The antient tang of scythe and hone.
Task for age, this setting-in
To let the reapers rightly begin
(Not today but tomorrow)
Across the long-since vanishd furrow.

Take it, sickle or 'sheen or scythe,
Who of us that bates his tithe—
Gift of golden work and sweat?
Harvest and hunger never met.
Riper the years grow while we labour.
Old Adam himself sets near us, Neighbour.
Swink and sweat, sweep and sway,
Gnarld are the fists that steadily
Inch the margin of corn away,
    Inch the margin of corn away,
        Inch the margin of corn away,

[xxxv]

The school is empty, and the street is empty,
And the stable's empty, and the only cool place
Is the church, empty, with its door ajar.
Houses are shut and all their kennels empty,
Shops in full sun and shops in shadow sleep.
'My shoes are dusty', thinks young Tom, aloud,

Alone and wonderstruck, making his way
Through unfamiliar sunlit moonlike silence,
Here, at own back-door, a trespasser,
Arrived to fetch a dinner-kit that stands
Where Mother'd left it, in the dark forsaken
Fireless kitchen—peeping Tom forlorn.

   A sea of corn has islanded all this;
Through the long epilogue stood green and tall,
Spared this year from laying with the thresh
Of heavy summer rain.
Through the shadeless afternoons it stood,
Swayed in the sun and the soft graceful wind,
Storing the vigour of the long succession
Of suns unclouded; till, the green all gone,
A hint of tawny fire began to burn
Deep in the congress of its nodding ears.
And still, good ripening drought continuing,
The sap from stalks dried out, and in a week
The fiery hint had gone again, and ripeness
Claimd all the casual. Now are men thigh-deep
In rustling foursquare ears, a millionfold;
And, scarvd against the sun, the golden girls
Stoop to twist bonds, and half-embrace each sheaf,
Then toss it from their arms. And urchins browse

On bread and apples in the acorns' shadows,
Or chase themselves like elves and interlace
Among the saplings of the woods, which fringe
The biscuit stubble with its sheaves unshockd.

[XXXVI]

Here, sleep, in a cradle of straw,
In a noonday shade and near to our labour,
Leaves thy screen, and fruitful earth thy neighbour—
While I to work, with thoughts for thee, withdraw.

Unclasp the poppy; lie with loosening fingers;
Sink, lashes, against the willing cheek;
Smile, dreaming—what innocence may seek.
The scythe rings; thy single lover lingers.

Here, sleep, in a cradle of corn,
With the sunlit air and thy breath blending,
For shadows shall lengthen soon, and, workday ending,
Thy newest wonder, the Moon, comes to be born.

Then, under Moon and Sun in heaven together,
On thy father's shoulder Home shalt thou ride,
Lofty, laughing down upon me at his side,
Thy weary mother, oh, thy happy mother.

[XXXVII]

Wheat from the ear; this is grave food indeed:
Not sweet, not luscious, not for gluttons this.
There's dire antiquity in gathering
This husky cylinder, in rubbing out
By palm on palm the wrinkled pearly grain,
Breathing away the chaff.

It is not hunger: it is some desire
Set deeper in the spirit, which is shared
Among all kinds of men: this is to taste
Earth's yield; the spartan answer to men's labour;
What goodness is. Here is the natural rite
Observed before religion got its gods:
Sons of the earth partaking of the sound
And natural substance of maternal earth.

Here is the sign each generation seeks,
The plain Consent, sufficing: We may live
If we will labour for it, or if others will;
Love, if we will not be greedy lovers—
A mother's justice, which accords our claim
Its justice also. Sober and dry. Enough.

[XXXVIII]

Now for the gypsy weather, scarved and flaunted,
Shortshrift of light, but free and of a tang,
Coloured all colours, from grass blue with frost
(Or dew like frost) at daybreak, to the deepest
Metallic violet-over-sulphur hearts
Of bryony girdles with their blood-drop berries
Slung over hedges.
Now apples rollick their last days on high,
And pickers' faces peer above them shouting
From topmust rungs, from tree to tree alive
With hands and heads and baskets.
Leaves lose their hold and fall about and die
And drift in paper money over the knees
Of beech-tree roots. Far-flung lie early evenings,
Bannered about the sky, where colour lingers

When the stacks are black long after star-time.

Nuts fall now rattling in the hollow woods,
And chestnut hedgehogs, split with heavy impact,
Scatter their trinities for Saturday scholars.
Now in remote and slightly haunted fields,
Where well neglected hedges riot hugely,
Bunches of varnished blackberries feel the crook
And fill the urchins' baskets.

Tidy lies the stubble on the hillside,
Though ragged at the foot that trespasses.

What's harvest when 'tis past? A serene yard
(The golden court of cocks and hens at leisure)
Square ricks and round ricks, all tight-thacked and barbered,
Quiet in windless honey-hinted sun.
Is this this year a-dying? This brown peace
That lolls about on sunny sides of spinneys
Enticing rabbits out,
This scatter of scarlet silence, this warm air
Stung with the ale-house smell of matting leaves,
This bribe that puts mere earnings out of mind—
Is this the year a-dying? Is it plenty?
Is it ripe age, that makes its will in liquor,
Born rich and richly multiplied? Adieu.

This autumn, too, the leaves have fallen,
Staining the trodden roads at home,
Playthings as ever for all the children,
For the trees, rest, for the land, loam.

Sometimes obedience that seems blind
Is best and has the longest sight,
And every day, stormy or quiet,
Of its deep nature turns to night.

Only as yet men hesitate,
Breaking their selfhood on the will,
Fiercely desiring a chosen change,
Revolt, and are unhappy still.

You lead us wrong; we trust you wrong;
You bid us here against our nature;
In herds of men no man is whole;
Leave us alone to find his stature.

Walking home through the woods after the rain
I saw the sun look coldly out
Under the levelled eyebrows of the clouds,
Giving desolate edge to all that did remain.
Much was gone now. Minds were held for winter
And summer-set and early dark, though now
The metal light
Leapt and glittered on wet boughs everywhere.
The world was empty of voice—no bird that sang—
Till this unstartled redbreast, high on a twig,
Above the horizon of lapsing light, who said
'Shee needn't be worried about mee!'
Suddenly, scornfully, finally,
And, when not even expected echo took him,
Echoed himself, bravely it seemed to me,
For he was all the mirth and all the birdsong
In the woods, after the rain. . . .
Floods lapped at our doorstep, flames on our hearth.

I listened to the wind in the dark, father,
To the drip where midnight rain comes through.
I leaned to that thought awhile: how he, the Sun
In his vault of perpetual silence, burns alone,
One other star slow-dying, self-consumed
Through the nightless space that drinks his glittering.

My infant son is asleep, man's new manchild
Compassed in cradle, and at peace meanwhile;
And all this universe darkness is reserved
Until in transient time, also, unnerved,
He, lost at midnight, listening to the wind,
Faces the horror of Space (and, like the Sun,
Uselessly). Then shall he find, as I do now,
With more reasoning than astronomy
That love lights on his heart, makes him rise up,
With gentle candle draws him close to the cradle;
Brings him to bed with comfort strange but sound.

Bring in a world, but fasten the door awhile;
Peel off the weather; settle, neighbour;
Let darkness rattle; let the gale roar;
Fetch forth the kettle.

As close lie my apples in hay, in store-room,
So snug in stacks lies your harvest, waiting.
Bring yourself in, man, muffle up the door—
No need to starve.

The weathercock cries in plunging starlight,
Croaking—hark—as he winds rustily;
For all that, steadfast our candles are—
Five of one mind.

We have calld up gales to our cosy wainscot,
Talkd of death, of birth, pleasantly—
Well, tomorrow's Monday, they say;
We're still on the earth.

It's much to turn, as we both of us did, John,
To a curtaind window, slapt suddenly,
To smile a wry gesture, and gossip on,
Fireglow lapt.

In a loud universe, in a wild nightmare,
The black wood roaring under comets,
That still we can differ by candle-light
Is worthy a wonder—

But I treasure a gale; for it whips the heart up,
Till timidest men feel gay, masterful—
Little weak men through wind and dark
Beetling their way,

Carrying lanterns, too. Nay, I'll out.
Yes, I will though, right to the church;
Now, my masters, let's take a bout with you!
Man, what a night!

[XLIII]

The moon, severe
In spite of her grin,
At bedroom window
Staring in—
The mortal, cold,
In spite of his clouts,
From bedroom window
Watching out—

No cloud on the steel.
Stars made dim
By moonlight, freezing,
Blinding him.
Silence contracts him;
The ash-grey ghost
Of moon's light
(On grass, like frost)
Over his knuckles
Claspt on sill
Lies, nakedly,
Marble-still.

Her calmness indeed,
Decoys him there,
Slows his pulse,
Stops his prayer:
Till Love could be little,
Faintly lost;
Death but a natural;
Time a ghost.
Here, unharnessed,
Transient, humbled,
One upon sight
Of All having stumbled,

A Man upon fact
Of No-Man gazing,
Will walk with a question
All his days,
Will bear with an answer
Words may not bind;
And yet be mortal...
[*He draws the blind.*]

Brought to pause for a minute, here, to breast
The cold, clean, bright, physical, earth—
Warmth of moving beginning at once to ebb
Into the east wind—here one of us said
To another, something of summer.
Incredible fact of summer, when these hedges,
When these barebone trees,
Were many mansions. But the thought, the faith,
Was past our skill, we could not now support it;
The cold besieging came too close; the day's
Reality demanded, to keep pace,

Our whole conception, next eternity.
So, striking the hard ruts, we shouldered on,
Cracking the grass bents, lest our frostbit blood
Should weakly crave us to the hearthside, sooner
Than health or manliness deemed decent. On—
And by-and-by limb-freedom came, and vigour;
The very sunlight might have been access
Of outer coldness; but we drew good breath.

  Then the woodman cheered us; his far-falling strokes,
Fateful for trees, and of enormous history,
Gave us an axe apiece, and prided us in men.

  There was no ploughing in such freezing, no
Efficacy now but in assenting;
Winter did all the soil-work, with frost's silent
Levers forcing the clods to iron.
We leapt on and up—an empty sky—
No birds, but one that huddled in a leaf-drift—
Till earth, mapped in unambitious sunlight,
Lay behind, around, before, weighed down
With rim of thick and leaden distances.
And, still, hale pride arose in animal triumph
As we struck, by step and step, across
The frost-baked field, the sloping hillside,
Its backward-diminishing furrows.

Brought to the hill-crest, ah, the sere wind swept
With a dry, roaring hoarseness across one's ears;
Drove home again the deadly truth of winter.
  Muffled up, two conquerors, elbow-limbed,
We stared across the outlined countries, dispeopled,
Swept of life clean by the pagan cold.
Save that a hedger immediately hereunder,
Rolling a tangled load of thorns aside,
Pitched them into the teeth and tongues of flames.
We heard the snapping rustle as they kindled.
Smokeless heat flickered over them,
The kingdom, parcelled out, quivering through
An invisible pillar twisted of wavering glass.
Then, turning full to the eyes of the sun,
Our steps fell into jolting; from clod to clod, down,
Down the steep slope again;
And we cried goodnight to the woodman, without stay,
Passing his empty courtroom by.
For deeper under the earth, this early evening,
By inch the vices of frost were twisting tighter;
Blackness as yet unseen threatened the sun;
The hollow ice munched on the darkening track;
The ivy leaves chattered about the ash-trees.

The world whitens softly;
As a dream's unreal,
With idle busy motion
The white bees wander and mingle
Eddying in swarms above,
Eddying in swarms below.

The still trees grow black and patient
Giving a lodgement to the snow;
Silence falls from the sky in pieces,
Settles, drifts on thought and places,
Grows.

For its beauty, terrible to see,
For its calm, a cruelty,
Answer of Heaven to all that the anxious
Heart would know.
As Truth to the mind; Sorrow to the merciful;
Quiet, as harmless sleep, but colder;
Falling, veiling, sifting, drifting
Snow.

Here might be shown an unpredicted season,
A cottage climate; proof of which suffices
That these four walls of Winter's narrowing jail,
Transmuted in the pause between two thoughts,
Buttress become and trusty battlement.
Hence, at a fire that needs but mortals' mending,
A warm epoch, by darkness rounded in,
The twice-tenanted peaceable hearth secures.

Each April is mighty and gentle, beckoning boughs
Jewelled with showers, trembling on to adventure;
But these four sheltering walls, with memory hung,
Against the ruin and starve of old December
Salve all our springs; and deep and quiet now
In proof is life whom it was ours to trust.

As mad as spring, to outward sage, appeared
Our barely calculated leap to space,
When two laughed back at winter, two that bartered
Caution care and ancient wisdom, boasting:
'Love will pay our tax and fetch our coals.'
This home we built before a brick was fired,
While ever the timber for its doors drew sap....

Whereupon You looked up; and quicker than truth,
Wiser than wisdom fares, your dream is established.
The substance-image of your character, this,
The tabernacle of your good life shared,
Tenderly hollowing from tempest dark
And envious frost as strong a citadel
As is by mortal life to be defended:
Each in each other's hope, and at one hearth
One mirth, one oath, and, when the need may be,
One grief borne well, without inquietude—
No hours not ours. Let doubters range and question
Of good and wicked, or what hidden sense—
If any—some score years of breath can make,
Faced by the certain curtain-call of death;
Such love, as poet master father here
Wrestling would thank, is known beyond the word
By its direct simplicity of liking:
As the substantial hearth, it cradles fire;
It is rock true, a refuge set in chaos,
Built into winter and by its hardness tempered,
This cave of manlight, clockless mantelshelf,
Where, for familiar currency of quiet,
We are waited on by Love the Lord of Heaven.

Long lost in paper work, in paper thought,
At last I looked up from my masters' table:—
Window to window across the ancient court,
Air is a moving net of flakes of snow,
All small alike, silently interlacing,
Wandering, waving, moving, delaying, turning,
Filling the great cube of space above the grass.

Often in spring, often in crystal summer,
Or in all clear seasons, as if the eyes were wings,
From a tedium of task have I resorted
To that wide well of still and resting air
In its motionless, its motionless attendance there,
For rest, refreshment, veritable example,
Of peaceful stillness, patient clarity.

But these small snowflakes tell, of that deceptive air,
A different character: the lines they weave
Are not a very movement of their making;
Innumerable and never-ending eddies
Trouble invisibly the air's transparency
Even in height of summer—even the innocent air
Deceiving me: never, never so still,

Never of that character which in my lack,
Searching widely through Nature, I
Had forced upon her of my spirit's greed...
Perhaps there is no rest; no air is ever still;
No air no heart no stranger ever still.

[XLVIII]

In winter he was born
In spring he died.
He saw no harvest,
For they crucified him.

He sees no harvest yet
(For the clerk that reaps is other)
Save some small weed ahead
At the wayside.

He is gone across our country
Once, and for all;
That which we hear in the heart
Was his footfall.

He has said of us, and fled,
What can never be unsaid;
He has eternally gone;
But we are changed to the bone.

[XLIX]

I heard the bells ring wisdom in—
I leapt from sleep to hear them ring—
My clumsy fingers buttoned fast—
The Air is in my mouth at last.

The crystal ghost is in the tree—
Calm has replied the present air—
Silence of love has set me free—
The noise of Christ is everywhere.

[L]

Now goodnight senses; aye
Now goodnight all;
Pull the curtains together,
Light the candle small,
Take worn-out shoe from foot,
Go quietly up to sleep
Though the ones we love delay,
Though the stairs be steep.

Go up, go up to bed,
Sir Self; for long has been
The day that ends at last.
Not what its riddles mean
Needs any longer tax,
Needs any longer bother
The fibres of a brain
That reason can no further.

'Brave' need we not expect,
But only willing be;
Of their own weight the eyelids
Will close presently;
And, then, in the silent time,
In the patient space,
May we hope once a holy whisper,
A serene face?

[LI]
This is the bare twig,
The iced weather around it,
With a brief purposeless sun
Lying in light upon
　　The branch above.

And still, doubly still
Falls morning on my ear
Because of the single shrill
Phrase that is bare and shapely,
That's trim and ruddy-breasted,
That's thorny as his bill
Who sits, in frost's white dust aloft,
Daring the winter-devil
     To work the worst of 's will.

I hear him marking silence out;
I catch the holly berries
Among their daggers laughing:
So doth a secret person
Laugh inward silently;
And the deeper driven, defiantly,
And striding fields away,
In bird-made strength a giant
He—like poverty, whose crumb
In time will probably come—
     Sees out this freezing day.

Now in profound of winter I render
My heart-born love of the sun.
There is no logic but the green earth, my dwelling,
Its rites and rigours compelling,
More than a mind can shun.

Then fly, light love, on wings away,
Wasteful as light spun into space;
Less than our lord the sun we know
Of the fall of an emanation:
His spring he comprehendeth not
(Which was and is to be till death
Earth's warming and her creatures' breath)
But burns untold, content, outgiving;
And may not I, the loving living?

Well may my kind of light light on
Some creature in a corner.
O flagstone frog, will you my planet be?
O bud of some town-dwelling tree?
O passer-by unwilling?
Move to an instinct ray that hastes
For the most part to waste, to waste.

Vast winter are the skies and dead
And vastly uninhabited—
The sun may burn in vain;
Yet sizeless earth, her apple interposing,
Finds a long winter closing,
Whose aconites, astir,
Shall tell, unknown to her,
In roots and folded buds and flowers
A pulse reviving;
Till I, a millionth man,
Look up and send my hope
On wings, and voyage forth,
Praising, with ignorant earth,
Her luminous sun,
His warmth and weal and shining.

[LIII]

Well the journeyman that can believe
The sight of hoarfrost in a winter tree
        Can believe anything.

✻

To my children

Take my hands from your eyes.
　Who can speak what you see?
Welcome tears where they rise—
　You were free; you are free.
Love and live as your liking is,
　Bold in earth, blest in skies;
For this harvest—we witness it.
　Take my hands from your eyes.

Printed in the United States
By Bookmasters